21st Century Leadership

Leadership

John R. Brophy

ISBN: 1499207611
ISBN-13: 978-1499207613

DEDICATION

The Freedom Tower in New York City was selected for the cover because I believe it symbolizes the resilience of the people and their leaders in the 21st Century.

The Freedom Tower was born of the tragedy of September 11, 2001. A day in which thousands of people were lost and the entire world was impacted. On that day and to this day existing leaders were challenged and new ones created as we all searched for answers.

There were many leaders lost that day and one in particular that I had the privilege of knowing and learning from was David Lemagne. David was an EMS Tour Chief in Jersey City where I had the opportunity to be guided by and learn from his leadership. On September 11th David was a Port Authority Police Officer who responded to the World Trade Center and was credited with saving countless lives. His spirit lives on in the people he saved that day and in everyone who had the privilege of knowing him.

To David and to everyone who lost their lives in New York, Washington, and Pennsylvania I dedicate this work.

CONTENTS

ACKNOWLEDGMENTS

Throughout my life and career there have been many people who have contributed to who I am. Many of these people are referred to in this book in the lessons they provided for me that I now have the privilege of sharing with others. I do so in the hopes of perpetuating the legacy of leadership they instilled in me.

To the people who served as positive examples of leadership, and even those who were an example of what not to do I say thanks for the memories and the lessons I learned from you.

To those closest to me who accept me for who I am and provide support and encouragement so that I can learn and grow from my failures as well as my successes I am eternally grateful. Specifically, to Jill (who is the reason there aren't more run-on sentences in this book) words cannot express how grateful I am for her unwavering support. And Dolph, Paul, Don, and Bill who are always there when I need their words of wisdom I could not ask for better friends.

To John Bredin for his support and encouragement of my writing in spite of our sometimes polarizing opposition to one another's political views I say thanks for being a lifelong friend.

Special thanks also to Jimmy Woods for his contribution of the cover photo of this book. Having worked with him for many years I know he is one of those 21st century leaders whose star is on the rise. Stay the course Jimmy and keep up the great work.

Finally, to Brian Molitor I would like to express my profound gratitude for taking the time to contribute a Forward for this book. I know that what I have learned from Brian has had a lasting impact on me as a leader and a person. I hope that his forward will give you a taste of the inspiration he has provided me that will leave you reaching for more.

John R. Brophy

Forward

Whether you are a coach, manager, teacher or supervisor, the art of leadership is essentially the same - Know where you are going, communicate to others, live by contagious core values and so on. However, the great divide for those in leadership comes not from the practices, but rather from the impact when one succeeds...or fails. The coach whose team loses a game gets to draw up a new game plan and try again. In the corporate world, failure likely means a lousy quarter and another try. For the teacher whose student falls behind, there is always extra credit, make up assignments and retesting. In these honorable fields, failure gets a mulligan...another try.

However, there is one group of leaders whose performance is measured by very different standards. For the men and women that lead in the complex world of EMS and Fire, the stakes are always set at the highest level...life and death. There are no extra innings when lives are at stake and seconds count. There are no instant replays to overturn a wrong call at the scene of a fiery crash. There is only life or death. Success or failure.

This begs the question: Why would anyone want to lead in such a field? EMS and Fire are not places to become fabulously wealthy and the job comes with long hours, little sleep, and lots of stress. So why...? The answer is simple, but not easy to comprehend. They lead because they must. They lead because inside each EMS and Fire professional is the deep, divine calling to sacrifice so that others may live.

John's book lays out the foundations needed for EMS professionals and others to live and lead by. He captures the heart of this ancient art of leadership and offers his insights in a way that is easy to grasp and apply. It is a worthy read, written by a pro with lots of experience. Well done, John.

Brian D. Molitor

1

DESIRE TO LEAD

Why lead? What drives those among us to step forward and seek to achieve things through their leadership? I believe it is that leaders have a vision and a desire to see that vision through. I think in many ways leaders not only see, but seek out opportunities that others do not. Leaders believe that good enough is not enough and certainly that anything less is simply unacceptable.

Thinking back to my very first leadership vision in EMS, I was 17 years old and had completed CPR, Advanced First Aid (the Red Cross ancestor of EMT training that was used as the centerpiece of training to be a member of a volunteer ambulance squad in New Jersey before EMT was more widely taught), and EMT. Yes I was an over-achiever of sorts as I took both the Advanced First Aid and the EMT training. In spite of having all the required training my hometown provided no means of using it on their newly formed volunteer ambulance squad. The minimum age requirement was set at 18 and I was 17.

Since no opportunity existed in my hometown, but I knew from the people I met during my training that other towns had a youth contingent to their volunteer ambulance squads, I set out to join a neighboring town's ambulance squad. I did so as a way to put my training to good use. Once onboard I gained experience in the field and learned from the elders of the organization how vital they felt the "youth corps" was to the future of their organization. They saw it as a mentoring and grooming opportunity to get people involved in community service at a young age and build a cadre of experienced and dedicated people who would be there to take the organization into the future once their time came.

For certain I was frustrated that my own hometown did not provide such an opportunity for the its youth to serve and to grow into the future leaders of this organization. As a result of my experience I gained renewed energy and enthusiasm to create an opportunity for the youth of my community in our hometown. Having originally taken the training out of a desire to learn and to serve I now had my first significant desire to lead.

There were others in my community who also had a desire to belong to the squad, many of whom also had the requisite certifications. The only thing holding us back was our age. In fact two of these individuals followed me to the neighboring town's ambulance squad to put their training to use and gain experience. Our desire to serve was also coupled with our desire to create a similar opportunity at home. While we served we gained much needed experience that later served to validate our credibility when we came forward with our proposal. Armed with our vision and experience we got together, held meetings, and drafted a proposal that was approved by the squad and adopted by ordinance of the Mayor and Council. This new law allowed for properly trained individuals between 16 and 18 to join, with parental permission, the newly formed youth squad. I was elected as the youth squad's first Captain and my two contemporaries who journeyed outside our hometown to find opportunities and experience rounded out the officer ranks as the youth squad's first two lieutenants.

That was back in 1982 and for more than 30 years the vision of a youth squad has provided countless opportunities for 16 and 17 year olds to serve their community and touch the lives of people in need. Their contributions to the community over the past three decades have been invaluable to the citizens and I know from my own experience that what they will take with them for the rest of their lives is priceless.

So, from my perspective and reflection of my own career I believe that the desire to lead comes from having a vision and a passion to see it through. I have found through reflection and research that while some cite generational differences as both a challenge and a cause for concern that there may be less to be concerned about than skeptics of today's youth seem to think. Let's face it, generational differences have always existed and will likely continue to exist long after we who inhabit the planet today are gone.

In his book, *The Catalyst Leader*, Brad Lomenick (2013) talks about three key areas that I can relate my own youth leadership experience to. From his conversations with young leaders he cites "the desire to lead now" as a common characteristic. He also found that social media and other technology have provided more opportunities to "start new initiatives, build a following, and make a difference" and contrasts it to the decades old normative path of plodding along to earn a "gold watch". Finally, he found that many young influencers (leadership is often very much about the ability to influence people to achieve a vision) seek to "find solutions to our world's problems and live lives that matter".

When I look back on what my lieutenants Steve, Tim, and I accomplished in 1982 as well as how and why we did it and compare that to the 2013 findings of Brad Lomenick about today's youth I see significant parallels. We had a desire to lead in the moment, we had a vision to start a new initiative that would make a difference and we sought to find solutions to the problems of "our" world and to live lives that matter. So to the "elder" leaders of the 21st century who are skeptics of today's youth I say take a look back to your first leadership vision and remember that you had skeptics and naysayers too. But I bet you didn't let them hold you back. Today's youth leaders are tomorrow's elders. I am not saying give them a free pass by any means. Challenge them, point out the flaws and concerns you see with their ideas that they may not have the benefit of experience to see, but do so with the purpose to help them analyze and explore their visions and ideas so that they achieve success. Don't just say no and discourage them as many elders did to us when we were full of ourselves with invincibility and new ideas.

2

LISTENING WITH EMPATHY & SINCERITY

Have you ever been talking to someone only to have them abruptly start looking at their phone or computer and respond to or initiate a text message or e-mail? Annoying right? Now ask yourself if you have ever done it. I bet most of us can answer yes and many who answer no are simply unaware they are doing it. Having been on the receiving end of this behavior at least one too many times I have become conscious of it and, while not perfect, do try to avoid it or at least minimize it. Think about the message it sends to the people you are with. Think about how you felt when it was done to you and realize that others may feel the same way and with the same right to that you had.

So why am I ranting on this apparent pet peeve that I, perhaps a bit hypocritical in so doing, am guilty of myself? Because I believe for as much as technology has provided us in the form of communications and other enhancements and efficiencies I believe it has taken as much or more away from us in the area of "people skills".   Instead of calling people we "text" them and instead of stopping by their office to connect on a project or idea we simply "send an e-mail".   Granted these options have their merit and their place.   But there are times I can't help but wonder if we have taken them too far and lost the ability to communicate and in particular actively listen to what others have to say.

Back when I was in my 20's, in a time when home computers with 512 kb hard drives were considered huge and portable phones were the size of a kid's lunchbox and only the more affluent had them I worked as one of four full-time staff people at a local chapter of a non-profit organization. The chapter had a couple of hundred volunteers including both operational volunteers out in the community and administrative volunteers in the office who answered phones and performed clerical and other such duties. One such volunteer was a woman named Dotti. She was a retired executive secretary that worked our switchboard one day a week. During her down time between phone calls she was very efficient and quite an asset to the organization in that she was able to manage any number of other tasks that needed to be done.

I think it started one rainy Tuesday afternoon when I came back to the office after a meeting. Having entered through the back door I needed to go through the kitchen area to get to my office. Dotti was there and was making herself a cup of tea. She asked if I wanted one and I said yes. I put away my coat and went back for my tea, from there she returned to her post at the switchboard and I sat in one of the waiting chairs nearby. We chatted that day and over time tea with Dotti became a regular Tuesday afternoon thing.

The punchline came a few months later when my boss went to her and asked her to perform some collateral duty or another while she was manning the switchboard. Dotti was working on something for me at the time and said to my boss that she would have to check with "her boss" (meaning me) to see if what she was working on could wait. My boss, who was the organization's director became a bit miffed and reminded Dotti that she was in charge and that her task would supersede the one I had given her.

With my office door right next to the switchboard I started thinking "oh boy, here it comes". Without a moment's hesitation Dotti politely, but firmly told the director that since she was a volunteer and the only one who made her feel appreciated was John. She also told her that everyone else just dumped stuff on her desk to do without taking the time listen to her or to even say thank you. She said that the only "extra" work she would do besides answering the switchboard was what John needed and if she (my boss) didn't like it that they would need to find someone else to volunteer on Tuesdays.

Needless to say, this resulted in quite the "evil-eye" from my boss as she glanced into my office. A few minutes later she called me on the phone and invited me to her office to discuss what had just taken place. I hadn't done it with any devious intent, but apparently my simply taking a few minutes every Tuesday to sit and listen to Dotti tell stories about her career, life, or whatever else was on her mind had earned me some significant loyalty. Those few minutes each week had clearly separated me from the others in her mind. Once my boss got past her initial reaction to Dotti's candor I think she too learned a lesson in leadership about the impact and importance of actively listening with empathy and sincerity.

Fast forward a few decades to an interview I was on that appeared to be going well, then all of a sudden one of the people interviewing me started answering texts or e-mails on their phone. I continued to engage with the others, who maintained the dialogue while thinking "OK, either I am already in or I have no chance whatsoever". Why else would a key player in the interview disengage mid-stream? Reflecting on that interview I can't help but wonder if that same person would have disengaged 20 or 30 years ago without the distraction of their cell phone. In so doing, I realized that just as I was a victim of their loss of focus, they were a victim of the technology we all use, sometimes to a fault every day.

As a result of the fact that I am a leader in the 21st century, but armed with the pre-technology interpersonal skills I have blended past and present in a number of ways:

1. When possible and practical I try to take a walk to the other person's office instead of simply firing off an e-mail when I have a question or need to discuss something.

2. If I have the choice of a phone call or a text message, I choose a phone call. Texts are great for letting someone know you are running late or confirming a quick fact, but when a quick conversation might better enable you both to flush out a subject try for the

phone call over the text. The result will not only get you the answers you need, it will build interpersonal skills and rapport.

3. When someone comes into my office and I am working on something that I can't immediately stop doing because I am in the middle of a thought, say in an e-mail for example, I say to them something like "just give me a minute so I can finish this up and give you my full attention".

4. When I go into a meeting I try (not always successful) and leave my phone behind so I won't be distracted during the inevitable low interest points meetings tend to have.

"Nothing stops the progress of an organization more quickly than leaders failing to listen" says Dr. Hans Finzel, author of *The Top Ten Mistakes Leaders Make* (2000). In short, the

21st century leader faces perhaps more potential distractions now than ever before. Therefore I believe it is imperative that leaders acknowledge and embrace the importance of listening, empathy, and interpersonal connections. Further, I would encourage my fellow leaders in all industries to be cautious not to use the technology designed to enhance communication as a substitute for making the connection that only the personal touch can accomplish.

3

AUTHORTY

When it comes to leadership, authority has three key elements. They are legal authority, moral authority, and earned authority. A leader that has all three is positioned well for success, but one who does not will have limitations placed on their ability to achieve their goals.

Legal authority is that which comes with an official position of responsibility. It is pretty much absolute. If you hold a certain position you have the legal authority that goes along with it. And there ends the simplest piece of the leadership authority puzzle. The other two key elements are not as "black and white". In fact they are often varying shades of "gray".

Moral and earned authority are elements of leadership that are more subjective and based in large part on what the people around the leader believe to be true. Think of a politician with high approval ratings vs. one with low approval ratings. Regardless of their ratings they have the "legal authority" to exercise the powers and duties of their office but find doing so easier when their approval ratings are high than when they are low. Political leaders with high approval ratings likely have earned them through their performance and strong moral behavior. On the other hand, those who see their ratings slip away often lose ground because they are not performing in a manner consistent with what the people impacted by their leadership believe to be necessary or appropriate.

But how does one "earn" authority as a leader? It goes back to a simple adage of the necessity to walk the walk, not just talk the talk. Leaders earn authority by saying what they mean and by meaning what they say. They earn authority as we discussed in the last chapter simply through listening and being sincere. They earn it by modeling the way and following through on not just the things that are important to them, but on the things that are important to their people as well.

Moral authority is gained by doing what's right no matter who is looking. I have heard it said that a leader leads by example, whether they intend to or not. If you think about that statement it is very true, whether the example the leader sets is good or bad they are setting an example just the same.

At one point in my EMS career a co-worker and I had the opportunity to apply for a manager-level position. I often tell this story as "the best promotion I didn't get". I do so because instead of skipping the supervisor-level I was able to spend a few years as a front-line leader. This was an opportunity I would not have gotten had I been the first choice for the manager's position. I held no ill will over his selection, in fact we worked well together as we complimented each other's strengths and weaknesses. And we are still friends to this day.

Perhaps even more important than the skills I learned in front-line leadership was the opportunity for me to experience first-hand the value, both short and long-term, of "earned" authority. I took on some of the more difficult collateral duties not just because they were areas I had an interest in, but more importantly because I knew they would help me become better prepared for the next manager-level position that opened up. I knew I could do more, but needed to "earn it" with my superiors, peers, and subordinates alike. Follow-through and attention to detail were things the people around me held in high regard and fortunately I found these things to be important as well. In large part I think we all had this same sense of their importance because they were not strong points of some of the people we had as our leaders over time.

I still remember about a week before I was promoted from supervisor to manager we were preparing a leadership retreat, our second in as many years. I was early helping to set up and make final preparations for a presentation I was giving as one of the speakers. A fellow supervisor caught up with me in the parking lot as I was bringing some supplies into the meeting venue and joked with me that I could slow-down and take a breath because I was the "heir apparent" for the manager's job. I smiled because I appreciated her knowing how hard I was working and making a point to recognize it. I also knew that my hard work was not just about getting the next promotion, it was about giving 110% every day and leading by example. It was about earning the authority that came with the supervisor position in the eyes of everyone around me so that I could be the most effective leader I could be.

When I think about moral authority in leadership I think about trust. John Salka (2004), now a retired Battalion Chief of the New York City Fire puts it succinctly when he says "trust is the only thing that makes leadership possible". He makes some key points to amplify this position when he reminds us that

> "without trust people won't share their best ideas with you, they won't stick with you when times get tough, and they won't open up to you and talk about the things that matter to them – their strengths, weaknesses, and values – all of which will help you get where they're coming from,

and ultimately to lead them where you all need to go".

As you can see, the desire to lead requires passion and sincerity along with an earned authority culminating in mutual trust. Like any relationship in any area of life, without trust the rest is in peril. This is why understanding that the three elements of authority we have been discussing in this chapter result in a level of trust. The higher the trust level the more readily a leader can execute their vision.

4

ACCOUNTABILITY
& RESPONSIBILITY

Leaders are not only accountable and responsible for themselves; they also have skin in the game when it comes to their people as well. Remember earlier when I said that leaders lead by example whether we intend to or not, well when it comes to accountability and responsibility the bar is even higher. Sure accountability and responsibility add to our moral and earned authority, but most importantly they are core elements of the effective leader.

It's been said that the behavior allowed will become the standard. Therefore, holding ourselves accountable for our own actions first will model the way for our people and create an atmosphere wherein expectations are clear. Leading by example allows a leader to more readily hold their people accountable since the "old school" do as I say and not as I do is no longer as effective as it once was.

The 21st century society demands more from leaders than ever before. People are more inclined to speak-up and speak-out when the behavior of their leaders does not meet their expectations. In fact, I wonder if their holding those of us in leadership positions to a higher standard isn't in some way driving our ability or inability to lead based upon how we measure-up in their view.

A few years back I was the manager of an emergency dispatch center. As such there were times when I would work the dispatch floor to cover an open shift. One Friday about mid-morning one of my shift supervisors came to me to discuss a staffing issue that was on the horizon for that night. Over the day or two preceding that Friday we had a number of people who were out multiple days with the flu. The supervisors and staff had done an excellent job of moving the pieces around the scheduling chess board to cover the openings, but had finally run out of pieces. They had everything covered except one dispatch position from midnight to 7 am. Knowing how hard they always worked, especially over the past couple of days I told the on-duty supervisor that I would go home a little early, take care of a couple of things and be back at midnight so that no one would be forced to work extra hours or short-handed.

Remember that promotion I didn't get? Well my understanding of the implications on the shift supervisor and the staff in this case was just one of the important perspectives I gained by not skipping a rung on the career ladder. This was one of many examples I believe helped me come to accept being the second choice as an invaluable positive and made me a more empathetic manager as well.

So, let's pick up with my coming back at midnight. I came in armed with my signature large coffee, which anyone who has worked with me more than a week knows it is a bit of a vice for me. As I enter the dispatch center I am greeted with the supervisor sitting at a dispatch console and the supervisor's console cleared in anticipation of my arrival. I got the gesture of respect for rank and such, but told the supervisor that it was his shift to run and I was just there to dispatch and help out as needed. He moved back to the supervisor console while I settled in, adjusted the console and my headset along with a few sips of coffee along the way. With that we were off to the races and as the call takers screened the calls I began dispatching them… "323 for assignment"….

After a short while there was a bit of "inappropriate chatter" on the radio by a couple of the field crews. Looking up at the radio identifier and determining who the culprits were I summoned one of them to call the dispatch center. When I answered the phone at about 15 minutes past midnight there was a short, but deafening silence followed by "um what are you doing there?" To which I replied "working, you?". With that they replied "misbehaving, sorry". I then asked if we needed to discuss this any further and they said no.

The crew knew what my expectation was, dating back perhaps to my time on nights as the supervisor of that very same tour. But why did they "misbehave" in the first place? Well when I was walking out in the morning I got my answer from the supervisor, who had also stayed until 7am on that particular morning.

In the elevator he thanked me for coming in and also added a thank-you for dealing with the radio etiquette issue. I saw a teachable moment about accountability and took the opportunity to share it with him. I started by asking him why he thought they changed their behavior when they knew I was listening, but felt it was OK when they knew he was listening. He said that it was because people knew what my expectations were and that I held people accountable to them. I asked him why they felt they could get away with it when he was working. He admitted that setting expectations and holding some people accountable was a bit of a challenge for him. We talked about a couple of ideas and I sent him home to get some rest with the reassurance that we would work on this together going forward.

While this story is in large part about the importance and impact of setting expectations and holding people accountable to them it is also an opportunity for me to acknowledge my responsibility for his coming up short in this area of his leadership development. Yes he was a supervisor and responsible for his performance and effectiveness, but so was I as his manager. In our conversation that morning and in others that followed I made sure he didn't feel like it was all his fault. Together we worked on strategies that fit his personality and leadership style that allowed him to become better at setting expectations and holding people, including himself accountable. Hopefully he also took away the message that I tried to get across about responsibility when he saw me give myself some of the heat when it came to his development as a leader.

In his book *The Speed of Trust* Stephen Covey (2006) tells a story about his childhood and how he was held accountable for keeping their yard "clean and green". His father didn't tell him how many times to mow or water it, which was up to him. The lesson he learned was that it is vital to take responsibility for results, not just activities. Although neither of us had read Covey's childhood lawn care story before this incident I think we arrived at a similar revelation… That while our approach might be different the important thing was the results. Had his son not achieved "clean and green" Covey would have had a piece of the responsibility, just as I did when my shift supervisor didn't achieve the desired results relative to radio etiquette.

5

EVERYONE'S A CUSTOMER

You are cruising along doing a good job. Deadlines are being met and organizational goals achieved. Then you come to work, check your voicemail and find a complaint from the public expressing their dissatisfaction with the service they received the night before.

Sounds like a Monday for sure, but no matter the day as a leader you have work to do to put fires like these out.

But why do these things flare up to begin with? Consider this...

I once received a complaint from a patient taken by ambulance to the hospital. It occurred on a cool but not cold spring day and the complaint was that the patient didn't feel well cared for because she was not given a blanket after being placed on the stretcher. When she asked the ambulance crew for one she said they exhibited frustration and told her, as they stood by her side in full uniform including a three-season jacket to keep them warm against the chilly spring air, that they did not have one available. They also tried to allay her concerns by telling her that it was only a short ride to the hospital.

When I was speaking with her she was polite, but for certain disappointed in what she believed to be sub-par service. I apologized profusely for her experience and the fact that we had not met her expectations. I also thanked her for taking the time to let us know that we had come up short so that we could use the opportunity this incident created as a catalyst for improvement.

Interestingly when I pulled up her record and reviewed it to determine who the crew was so that I could get their side of the story I found that had she not called us about this failure of "people" care that her "patient" care met all clinical and operational perspectives. Response time was good, full assessment with multiple reassessments at appropriate intervals, appropriate interventions based on findings, and so on. In short we arguably had appropriate "patient" care from a strictly clinical perspective, but came up short on our "people" care (which by the way could have easily impacted her "patient" care had the need for warmth been more clinically necessary). But it was more than just the blanket; it was that they were frustrated either by her request or by the fact that they could not honor it.

So when I went to speak with the crew to get their take I found out that they and other crews had been asking their manager for more blankets for some time with limited success.

They said that sometimes the manager was right on top of it, but others the manager seemed to not see the importance. They felt the manager was aloof about it and surmised from their conversations with them that the warmer the weather got the less important this seemed. They said "all the manager cared about now was getting the A/C's running because "more crews were complaining about being too hot than were complaining that the patients were too cold."

I apologized to the crew on behalf of the organization that we had let them down by not providing something so simple as a blanket. More importantly, I apologized for our not being responsive to their concerns. As we ended the conversation I assured them I would follow-up with their manager and told them to keep me posted and let me know how this issue went.

I called the manager and asked them to meet me at my office. While I was waiting I took a quick minute to add a calendar event about two weeks later. That calendar event was set as my reminder to reach back out to the crew. It is a simple trick I use to make sure I remember to follow-up and have found it to be as helpful as it is simplistic. As time goes by and other challenges arise it's nice to know I have a safety net to remind me to touch base with one person or another and make sure that their needs are met. It also provides an opportunity for them to feel their concerns are important and have not been forgotten.

Let's face it, if someone told us they were going to do something and a few weeks went by and we didn't see results would we bother calling them back? Or might we just chalk it up to just another of those people who doesn't do what they say they will? By me making a point of follow-up it provides me a chance to check progress, make sure things are going as promised, make adjustments if needed, and most importantly send the message that what is important to them is important to me.

If the manager who stopped focusing on the blankets in favor of the air conditioning were receiving the complaint about the blanket in the scenario I just laid out do you think they would have looked for the root cause or just assigned blame? Do you think their analysis would have lead them to shine the light of scrutiny on themselves?

I ask these questions as a means of reminding us about the importance of leadership responsibility and that as a leader everyone is a customer. Additionally, we need to remember that our people will tend to emulate us. Meaning for the purposes of this chapter (although it applies to everything we do or don't do) that if we provide good customer service to them that they will be more likely to provide good customer service to others.

Back in the 1970's the White House, during the Ford Presidency, commissioned a study of customer service and its impact on businesses in America. In her book *Your Call is not that Important to Us*, Emily Yellin (2009) says that "this study, and others, showed a significant impact on loyalty by customers who had a bad experience and were unhappy with their treatment".

As leaders if we provide poor customer service to our people their loyalty to us and the organization is going to wane. So too is their customer service to our clients and others they interact with on our behalf. When this occurs it is largely our fault because we have poorly modeled the way. But if we set the bar high for ourselves and make a conscious effort to follow-through on promises and hold ourselves and our people accountable we are setting ourselves, our people and our organizations up for success in the 21st century.

6

EVERYONE'S A LEADER

If you currently hold an official leadership position think back to before you first held one before answering this question:

Did you have ideas that you thought could better the organization?

For those reading who have yet to hold an official position of leadership answer this question:

Do you have ideas that you believe could better the organization?

I am willing to bet both groups had the same answer and that the answer was the same…yes.

Now think about the people around you in your organization. Do they have ideas they believe would be of benefit? I bet they do as well, even if sometimes some of their ideas are contrary to yours.

Does everyone in your organization have some level of influence (whether positive or negative in your view) over the people around them? While on the surface sometimes it may not seem so in all cases, I would bet if we truly looked we would find in both the obvious and not so obvious cases that the answer is yes.

Well guess what; in its simplest form leadership is vision and the ability to influence others. So if everyone has ideas (vision) and some level of influence then everyone is a leader. Granted not everyone has 20-20 vision relative to their ideas and some are bad influences, but then I never said everyone was necessarily a good leader. We need only look at history to prove that.

Back in my early days as a firefighter (probably sometime in my first 5 years) I recall attending Firefighter II class with a mix of people. Some with my own level of experience and some with a couple more years than me as well. As with any industry, the fire service is continuously evolving and we all learned a few "new" ways of doing things. Ways that surely were not taught in Firefighter I when I took it. And ways that may or may not have been taught to the more senior "elders" of our department.

One particular item was a hose load called a "minuteman" which was designed to be quickly pulled from the fire apparatus one "man" (firefighter). When we used it a few times in training we liked it and during our drives (about 30 – 40 minutes each way) back and forth from the fire academy we discussed wanting to try it back at the firehouse. So we approached the officers and a few of the "elders" and were afforded the opportunity to show them what we learned. But it was not all peaches and cream. We had a mixed audience in the people we wanted to convince to use this "new" idea. Their enthusiasm level ranged from genuine interest in seeing what we were talking about to reluctant skepticism to "we never used to do it that way" and there is no reason we should now.

So, after a couple of weeks of taking our "vision" and adding our persistence to influence them to at least let us show them we had our chance. As I recall it was a Sunday morning (our typical day for chores and drilling around the firehouse). We pulled the hose off the engine and re-packed it like we were shown. We even tried it once (a last minute rehearsal if you will) before bringing them outside to watch. We were ready, but were they?

So we did our demo and showed them this "new" idea. Some of our audience thought it was anticlimactic and in typical firehouse form let us know what they thought. Others were quiet. And others started saying things that started with "that's nice but what if you have to do this or that?" Since the ones asking the what if questions were the ones with the most authority (legal and/or earned) and as such the ones we absolutely had to convince we re-packed the hose again and again. We did it so we could pull it back off and show them how it will work in each of the "what if's" they presented.

Finally, they ran out of questions. Thankfully for our idea it wasn't before we ran out of enthusiasm. I believe a large part of us being to maintain our enthusiasm and belief in our idea was that each time they threw a situation at us it worked! At the next meeting it was announced that we would be making the switch to the "minuteman" hose load.

When I look back on this I think about how some of the "elders" had been fighting fires before I was born. I was the youngest in the group that attended that Firefighter II class where we learned the "minuteman". They had wisdom from their years of service. But when I hear stories about some of them that pre-date my time as a firefighter one of the many things that people remembered about their "younger days" was how they were always signing up for classes and taking the time to learn as much as they could about putting out fires. We were to them what they were to the "elders" of their youth. They were leaders before, during, and after they had titles and so now are we.

Fast forward about 20 or so years, my peers and I have transitioned to "elder" status. Along comes one of our younger members, fresh out of Firefighter II (the new and improved version) to tell me that our "minuteman" is packed wrong. Holy cow did I have a flashback! A young guy telling an old guy that hose is packed wrong, where had I seen that before?

The reality was that he was not entirely mistaken. Since first deploying the "minuteman" hose packing strategy we had purchased a new fire engine, one on which we could not pack the "minuteman" as originally designed. Talk about disappointment, was there finally a flaw found in our precious "minuteman"? We were undaunted and determined to find either a different way to pack the hose that was as good (in our minds at least) as the "minuteman" or a new way to pack the "minuteman". We came up with what I now call "minuteman 2.0". We had found a successful way to keep the benefits of the "minuteman" (nozzle and extra hose at the doorway) without the pitfalls (a pile of hose looking like spaghetti at the side of the fire engine) of a traditional hose pack. In a word, we had "success".

It was time for another trip outside to the parking lot on a Sunday morning. This time instead of being the youngest guy there, I was the oldest. Boy how time flies! We go set-up and I showed him why "minuteman 2.0" was not the same as what he was shown at the fire academy. Then I let him pack it how he thought it should be wondering if "minuteman 2.0" would stand the test of time, but open to the possibility that he might have "minuteman 3.0" ready for release.

We ran through his version of how it should be done a few times and it didn't work, 2.0 had stood the test of time. But more importantly we both had an opportunity to learn. He was encouraged to try out his idea and in the process became more familiar with the existing set-up in. He was better prepared for when he would have to use it on an actual fire. I was able to encourage him and others within the department to bring new things forward so that they can be tried before being dismissed out of hand. In so doing perpetuated the importance of staying current and blending tradition with progress that I was taught by the "elders" of my youth.

In his book *Learning in Action* David A. Garwin talks about the impact of an environment that is psychologically safe for people to pursue the benefits of new approaches has on an organization's ability to grow. From the stories I was told, my "elders" in the firehouse faced more resistance from theirs than my contemporaries and I faced from them. Hopefully I was able to be more receptive in this case and others to the future "elders" of the organization. At the same time reinforcing the importance of the balance between tradition and progress. A balance commonly referred to as "best practices" that has found great success in EMS and other industries. One which I know that if implemented correctly by our 21st century leaders will serve to lay a solid foundation for the fire service of the future.

7

PERMITTING IS PROMOTING

When behavior is allowed it is perceived by that person as acceptable. When others see the behavior being allowed they too perceive it as appropriate. In the early 1900's Ivan Pavlov saw this with his dogs and we continue to see it today as leaders in the 21st century.

Over time groups develop norms and in so doing establish an atmosphere of conformity. It is up to the leaders, both formal and informal to model the behavior expected and to not allow deviations considered not in keeping with the expected behaviors and culture of the organization to occur.

An example comes to mind of an evening at the firehouse after a training drill. The behavior expected is that after the practice session or class is over all members assist with the routine periodic clean-up of the firehouse before leaving unless permission is granted by an officer. It is a simple, straight-forward, and reasonable expectation in my view. In this case however one of the members apparently left before clean-up was complete and did not check-out with an officer.

The Captain called the member on their cell phone and asked if everything was OK. He first asked about their welfare. I believe because he knew it was out of character for the member and because he was genuinely concerned. Once he knew the member was OK he provided a choice. The member could come back to the firehouse or forfeit credit for the training that they completed. No yelling, no brow-beating, no autocratic demand to return. A choice was given and the member had the option to determine the next step in their own behavior.

A few minutes later the member came back into the firehouse. By this time however the clean-up was complete and we were free to go. But as is the case in many firehouses, some of us were lingering telling stories and watching TV. The member reported to the Captain who thanked them for coming back and told them that clean-up was complete and they could go. Result: Lesson learned and expected behavior reinforced.

The member who left learned a lesson and was given an opportunity to choose to behave in accordance with expectations or not. The members who were there, myself included, saw that the expected behavior applied to everyone. We also saw that the Captain was a fair and reasonable leader, and one who held his people accountable.

Seeing this I was reminded of a similar situation and approach taken by one of my EMS supervisors who discovered that I had unintentionally taken a portable radio home after my shift. He called me after I arrived home and told me I had to return it that night. With a 45 minute to an hour drive each way to and from work this was a 2 hour mistake. We both knew there were extra radios and that I was due back in the very next morning. So why make me come back? Was it just because he could? Knowing him I do not believe that to be true, but I am sure we all know leaders who would for just that reason. Knowing him I believe he did so to reinforce the importance of professionalism that was expected of us.

In both cases expectations were not met. In both cases the leaders involved took action to not only address the issues of the individual incidents, they reinforced the importance of the desired behavior in the process. They created discipline in us without formal punishment. In both cases scolding and/or written disciplinary action could have been their leadership tool(s) of choice. Instead they opted for an approach that would have both short and long term results.

As time went on and I moved through different areas of growth and responsibility in my career I have used similar approaches with a pretty good level of success. One such time was when I took over leadership of 4 divisions of an EMS agency. Upon doing so I was obviously given expectations from my boss that along with my own observations served as the basis for my developing an action plan to reinforce what was currently working and improve where opportunities presented themselves. My approach was keep the good, correct the bad, and add some new.

All of the divisions were using electronic patient care reporting, but one had a significantly higher utilization of paper patient care reports. This was in spite of all areas having the same technology and a common IT infrastructure and support system. When I met with the supervisors they told me that the crews told them every day that they had IT issues (computers didn't work, bad charging cords, batteries that didn't hold a charge, and other similar things) that were preventing them from using the computers.

I randomly checked a few computers and they were working fine, yet the crew's whose computers I checked also had a stack of paper patient care reports for the same shift. While I was sure that some of the issues were actually IT related I believed the lion's share of the issues were employee behavior that was permitted by the leadership of the division.

Based on my findings I gave my next steps some thought and recalled the lesson I learned with the portable radio. I realized that I had an opportunity to manage expectations. The next day I checked with IT to make sure they had some spare computers, batteries, and cords. I did so first because I knew we were going to find some valid IT issues and I wanted us to be prepared. Once I had infrastructure support confirmed to be in place I moved to the behavior modification piece of the puzzle.

The issue was significant and had an impact on the quality of the documentation we provide to hospitals and others who receive our patients. It also impacted our ability to be reimbursed appropriately for the services we provide. Given these considerations I approached it as a performance improvement project. I put the word out to the supervisors that we were going to be engaging in an initiative to identify and correct the underlying issues that were impacting the ability to use the electronic patient care reporting system in their area. I let them know that IT was prepared to give them full support with a high priority on any IT issues they discovered. I also told them that any other issues we found would be addressed once we discovered and validated them.

It was important to set expectations and collect data on what was happening so that we could fix the root cause of any issues. As such, the supervisors were instructed to obtain a paper incident report from every crew every time they could not use their computer on a call. This accomplished two things. First it empowered the staff to report every issue on every call in writing thereby holding us (leadership) accountable to fix any issues reported. It also assured that we had timely information on what was impeding their ability to utilize the technology that three other divisions were not experiencing. Additionally, much like the Captain and the member who left early after drill, it allowed crews who were simply opting not to use the electronic patient care reports to choose to continue to do so or not. They also knew that whatever reasons they put down for not using the electronic system would be checked and verified as part of the performance improvement project.

Within a few weeks we went from 750 or more paper charts a week to less than 50. While we did replace a couple of batteries and a handful of chargers not a single computer needed to be replaced. Most importantly however, the issue was resolved without a single formal disciplinary document being written.

Obviously this approach will not work in every case with every individual, but when the opportunity presents itself the 21st century leader should consider reinforcing organizational expectations through a balance of empowerment and accountability.

In *Psych 101* Paul Kleinman (2012) describes a phenomenon called social facilitation. He says "the most basic theory regarding social psychology is that when a person is alone he or she is more relaxed and not concerned about the appearance of their behavior". He continues the thought by telling us what happens when even "just one other person is added to the equation behaviors begin to change and people become more aware of what is going on around them".

In this case the issue started because one, then another, then still others who chose not to use the electronic system were introduced to those who were trying to do so. Over time the behavior shifted and the result was over 750 instances (most of which were behavior based) where the system was not being used.

Flipping the behavior back the other way involved the application of the same concept. First one, then another, then others were added to the mix that decided it was a better choice to be compliant with the expectations of the organization.

In the final analysis, leading people is not easy but when we understand how they think and behave as individuals and in groups we can better guide them where we need them to go. We can do this by establishing expectations, reinforcing positive behavior, and not allowing inappropriate deviations.

8

INTEGRITY

There may not be an "I" in team, but there is one in integrity.   So before we talk about teams (Chapter 9) let's spend this chapter discussing integrity as a means of understanding both its individual and collective value.   When we project ourselves we say things like "I am going to...",   "I should have...", and "I did...". Thinking of this simple fact I boil it down to "I is for Integrity and I means me".   If I is for integrity and I means me then by taking care of me the I of integrity is taken care of as well.

 In short, integrity is an individual responsibility. If everyone takes care of their individual responsibility in the variety of situations we all encounter then the ethical dilemmas we face will be simple to address. Remember I said if and as we all know if can be a powerful word as well. But don't be afraid, the more you put integrity first the more comfortable you are with it and the easier it will be when those more challenging situations and people come along.

Thinking back over 20 years ago I recall the treasurer of my fire company coming to me with a check we received as a donation. It was around the time of our annual fund drive and could have easily been caught-up in the numerous donations we received over a period of weeks each year. However, the treasurer noticed a note attached to it thanking us for the care we provided to one of their family members when they called the ambulance. This was important because our fire company did not provide ambulance service, but the other fire company in town did.

When he saw the note he realized that the donor was sending the check and the thanks for something we hadn't done and therefore we should not accept the donation. I thought it was a great catch and more importantly a measure of his integrity that he knew it was not rightfully ours and reported it. The next day I took the check and the note to the other fire company and gave it to their officer in charge. In so doing we set the example and "paid it forward" by doing the right thing.

He could have easily not read or comprehended the note. Or, worse yet, he could have discarded the note and deposited the check along with the rest and no one would have been the wiser. But his integrity would not allow it. It was a great example then and remains so today.

Let me ask you this... Can anyone teach integrity and ethics? I say yes. Let me explain why with a hypothetical....

A father is taking his son to the amusement park where children under 5 get in for free. On the way to the amusement park he strikes up a conversation with his son and says "I know you turned 5 a couple of weeks ago and you are very proud of it, but dad is short of money this week so I need you to tell the person at the ticket booth that you are 4."

Is he teaching his son about integrity? You bet he is! But what lesson is he teaching?

Integrity builds trust. It also adds to that moral and earned authority we talked about a few chapters back. Building trust is a slow and steady process, like the turtle in the race with the rabbit. Losing trust happens as fast as the rabbit can run in the wrong direction. With the trust diminished it will then take the turtle even longer to regain their previous position if they have to start as far back as the rabbit fell.

Think about public figures (elected officials, celebrities, etc.) and look at how long it takes them to build a career and how quickly they fall from grace when a "scandal" erupts. Just search "celebrity scandals" or "political scandals" on the internet for the most up-to-date list. Unfortunately is ever-changing. Another unfortunate reality is that some of the people accused in scandals are innocent, yet perception sets in from the front page story and "breaking news" coverage. And where does the retraction land? For sure it doesn't get as much coverage as the original "breaking news". Unfortunately the damage is already done.

When it comes to integrity Badaracco and Ellsworth (1989) remind us...

> "Very often the main problem is simply a lack of courage. Not the valor of grand, heroic acts, but determination and honesty practiced daily in small situations and familiar dilemmas of managerial life; the courage to do and say what one believes to be right, rather

than what is convenient, familiar, or popular; the courage to act on one's vision for his or her organization."

Their position reminds me of a situation when a former boss of mine took me with them to meet a client. I was in a new role in the organization and it was the first time I was meeting them. At the same meeting my boss had to tell them that we had not met our one of our targets the previous month. When explaining what happened and apologizing he told them that while it was a significant issue we had a plan to correct it going forward. He said he hoped that they would allow us that chance, but if they didn't he would rather lose the contract for poor performance than for dishonesty (ie not telling them about the issue).

As we were driving back to the office he explained that if we ever lost that contract or any other that we could go to other clients and say "yes we made a couple of mistakes over there, but we have learned from it and here is how we will prevent it from happening with you". He finished his point by talking about losing a contract for dishonesty. He said we really can't go to a potential client and say "yeah we lied to them but we promise not to lie to you". It was a powerful lesson in integrity and set a clear "walk-the-walk" example of what was expected of me in my new position.

So remember I is for integrity and I means me. When you look in the mirror in the morning ask yourself what kind of example am I going to set today? Before you go to bed ask yourself whether or not you met the expectations you set the last time you looked in the mirror. I think of it like this…

The only one I have to look at in the mirror is me. Do I like what I see?

9

BUILDING & ENHANCING TEAMS

Remember earlier how we spoke of the importance of trust in leadership? Well trust plays a key, in fact pivotal, role in teams. Whether it is sports teams at any level, groups of employees in an organization or department, or a neighborhood group planning community events all are brought together by their common goals, but held together by their trust in one another. It is the glue that holds cohesive teams together.

A couple of months ago I was returning an air pack to its bracket on the fire apparatus I had responded to a "working" house fire on. As I was doing so I thought about the trust factor that exists in the fire service and how it is woven in the fabric of what we do. Think about it, a few hours earlier I left my house and responded to the fire station. I donned my gear, and took my place on the engine. Without hesitation I turned on the air, checked the gauges, and was ready to go in with whoever arrived next into a dangerous situation. Why was I able to have that mindset? In a word, trust.

When an atmosphere of trust exists and everyone is accountable not only to their leaders but to each other the opportunities for a team to flourish are abundant. In contrast, when people in an organization lack trust in one another and their leaders those opportunities are generally few and far between. Patrick Lencioni (2002). Author of *The Five Dysfunctions of a Team* sums it up like this... "in the context of building a team, trust is the confidence among team members that their peers' intentions are good, and that there is no reason to be protective or careful around the group".

What I would like to do now is contrast Lencioni's (2002) five dysfunctions with the five elements of Maxwell's (2003) "Law of Countability", which he sums up as the teammates ability to count on one another when it counts.

First, according to Lencioni (2002) the five dysfunctions are:

1. Absence of Trust

2. Fear of Conflict

3. Lack of Commitment

4. Avoidance of Accountability

5. Inattention to Results

Next, according to Maxwell (2003) the five elements of what he calls countability are:

1. Character

2. Competence

3. Commitment

4. Consistency

5. Cohesion

Now, take a look at your organization (and don't forget about a long look in the mirror before you do). Do you have more dysfunctions or more "countability" items? Your answer to that question will set the stage for what you and your team need to do next. Either way you will have work to do. I suspect you and your organization will fall into one of the following three situations:

1. Lots of dysfunction and little "countability"

2. Lots of "countability" and little dysfunction

3. A somewhat balanced mix of both

If you and your team are in situation 1 there is plenty of work to do, but quite likely getting started will prove very challenging. The reality in this situation is that someone needs to step forward and break some eggs to make an omelet in a situation where no one wants breakfast food. It is not going to be easy, in fact at times it may seem almost pointless – almost like running a marathon with cement shoes on. But the reality is that it will be a marathon and there will be times of pain and frustration. Like a marathon runner you will just need to push past the pain to be successful.

Situation 2 is a bit more palatable. You have already made your omelets to order for most, but some still don't understand that it is breakfast time. This situation may in some ways be even more challenging than the first in that you are most of the way to a healthy team already. The challenge here becomes convincing people that as good as you already are that you can be even better if you put in a little extra effort.

Situation 3 is often a result of polarization that has resulted from a series of reluctant give and take compromises in which many were not truly happy with the results. There are lines in the sand that have been drawn and a lot of well functioning silos within the larger organization that are cohesive and have trust within them. Unfortunately they often lack trust in other people or the other silos they work in.

Often biased information results in learning disabilities that hinder an organization's ability to learn and grow. David Garvin (2000) discusses this in his book *Learning in Action* and lists the three learning disabilities as:

1. Blind spots

2. Filtering

3. Lack of information sharing

To me these three organizational learning disabilities contribute to, if not create in some cases, the dysfunctions we discussed earlier. To summarize Garvin's (2000) work in these three areas let's look briefly at each:

1. Blind spots often occur when we limit our search for information to that which supports our preexisting views.

2. Filtering occurs when critical information is downplayed because it is not in keeping with preexisting schemes or frameworks.

3. Lack of information sharing occurs when each functional fiefdom keeps data within their silo, whether intentionally or not. As a result limits the data the other areas receive while at the same time limiting the data the other areas share with them.

In all cases one must build on strengths to overcome weaknesses. I have found that where there is conflict there is energy. I find this important because if you can successfully turn some of the negative energy to the positive side you will have created a win-win. What I mean by win-win is that you will have eliminated a negative and created a positive.

To use a football analogy it would be like an interception in the end-zone that is run back for a touchdown – it is a 14 point play. You will have taken 7 points off the opponent's score and added 7 to your own, thereby creating a 14 point shift in the score. OK, if one or both kickers miss the extra point it is a 12 to 13 point shift, but you get my point…the shift is in your favor.

But where do we begin? I suggest you use a triage approach. Triage is a French word that means to sort and for those in the medical profession you will be keenly aware of this concept. In the field triage uses a "start where you stand" approach and work from there. So, within your organization I say "start where you stand". Identify the positives that you need to reinforce and solidify, then identify and prioritize (triage) the negatives and then start "treating" them.

10

UNDERSTANDING & LEADING CHANGE

As we wind down our journey through my thoughts on 21st century leadership lets reflect on the first chapter where we discussed the desire to lead. You will recall that an often present element in one's desire to lead is a vision to change something for what they perceive to be a better way. With this aspect of what drives leaders to lead it is important that we take a few moments to discuss change.

When I think back to the resistance and hurdles my contemporaries and I faced at the time when we were trying to convince others to start a youth squad I recall many of the elements of change I studied and have seen in other cases throughout my life and career. The reality is that we were successful because we had a worthy vision and a desire to see it through. I bet if we understood some of the aspects of change that we are about to discuss in this chapter that we may have had a few less hiccups along the way. On the flip side while not making some of the mistakes we did we would also not have had the same opportunities to learn and grow from them. I guess what I am trying to say is this....sometimes mistakes and even downright failures are an invaluable part of learning and growing and ultimately lead to even bigger successes in the future.

A few years back I had a direct report come to me with a very profound idea. My reaction was, in a word "wow". He smiled, and in his trademark self-deprecating manner said "I guess even a blind squirrel finds a nut every now and again." Sometimes as leaders we have to not take ourselves too seriously as Dan did in describing himself as a "blind squirrel" because it helps keep us grounded. And when it comes to change and new ideas we need to realize that sometimes we too can be "blind squirrels" who at times simply have an "ah-ha" moment. But, more importantly we need to accept and assist the "blind squirrels" around us in finding their vision. We need to create an environment in which they are not afraid to share it.

After Joan Lunden left Good Morning America (GMA) she embarked on a journey of finding and creating her new normal. Among her accomplishments since leaving GMA was a book she wrote called *A Bend in the Road Is Not the End of the Road* (1998). It is about dealing with change and some principles she discovered and used along her journey of change. In her book she writes "We cannot avoid change. It is the one constant in our lives, yet it produces the greatest amount of fear."

Since we cannot avoid it, let's take these last few pages to try and understand it a bit. Once we have a better understanding of change we can end with some strategies on how to lead change.

In its simplest form, change has three phases – the current state, the state of transition, and the desired state. The first and last phases are easy compared to the state of transition. The first is where we are and the last is where we want to be. The state of transition, as Conner (1992) puts it is a state that is uncomfortable as "no one likes existing in a state of limbo because the in-between periods in our lives are

filled with instability, conflict, and high stress".
It is because of this that leaders must
understand change and the reactions people
have to it. Leaders must account for it in their
planning and execution of the achievement of
the desired result.

Let's take a look now at some of the reasons
people resist change. There are many reasons
for sure, but for purposes of our conversation I
am going to rely upon a list put forth by
Professor Gary Yukl in his text *Leadership in
Organizations*.

1. Lack of trust

2. Belief that the change is unnecessary

3. Belief that the change is not feasible

4. Economic threats

5. Relative high costs

6. Fear of personal failure

7. Loss of status and power

8. Threat to values and ideals

9. Resentment of interference

Looking over this list we see a few items we have already discussed in other areas. For example, trust keeps coming up over and over as it relates to leadership. The importance of trust is perhaps one of the biggest take-away point from this book as it relates to leadership.

I would guess, if not bet that each one of us has either seen or felt one or more of these resistances to change in some aspect of our lives. Seeing it in others is one thing, but reality is that the cases in which we felt it best reinforce the fact that Yulk (2006) is correct that these reactions to change are not simply academic.

Knowing and having even experienced some, if not most of these resistances allows us as leaders to be better prepared to account for them when we embark on a mission of change. Unfortunately no matter how well we prepare the resistance will still be there. But that does not excuse us from doing so, it requires us to so that we can minimize the gap between the current status and the envisioned or desired status.

In looking at this list I see five key elements of leadership that must be employed when leading change:

1. Building and sustaining trust

2. Actively listening to the people around you

3. Actively communicating the vision and the why (reasons for change) behind the what (change itself)

4. Knowing and understanding your people

5. Knowing your organization and your industry

In short, this list boils down to the fact that a leader must do their homework and take the steps necessary to achieve the desired result with the least amount of disruption during the transition.

Leadership is the catalyst that takes us from the lessons of the past through the challenges of the present. It prepares us to confront the future with an open mind and an eye towards continuous improvement of who we are and what we do.

REFERENCES & RESOURCES

Badaracco, Jr. , J. L. & Ellsworth, R. R. (1989) *Leadership and the Quest for Integrity.* Boston, Massachusetts: Harvard Business School Press.

Conner, D. R. (1992) *Managing at the Speed of Change.* New York: Villard Books.

Covey, S. M. R. (2006) *The Speed of Trust.* New York, New York: Free Press.

Finzel, H. (2000) *The Top Ten Mistakes Leaders Make.* Colorado Springs, Colorado: Nexgen.

Garvin, D. A. (2000) *Learning in Action.* Boston Massachusetts: Harvard Business School Press.

Kleinman, P. (2012) *Psych 101.* Avon, MA: Adams Media.

Lencioni, p. (2002) *The Five Dysfunctions of a Team.* San Francisco, CA: Jossey-Bass.

Lomenick, B. (2013) *The Catalyst Leader.* Nashville: Thomas Nelson.

Lunden, J. (1998) *A Bend in the Road Is Not the End of the Road.* New York: William Morrow and Company, Inc.

Maxwell, J. C. (2003) *The Indisputable Laws of Teamwork Workbook.* Nashville Tennessee: Thomas Nelson, Inc.

Salka, J. (2004) *First In Last Out - Leadership Lessons from the New York Fire Department.* New York, New York: Penguin Group.

Yellin, E. (2009) *Your Call is not that Important to Us.* New York, New York: Free Press.

Yukl, G. (2006) *Leadership in Organizations.* Upper Saddle River, NJ: Pearson Prentice Hall.

PHOTO CREDITS

Cover: James R. Woods

Author Photo: Jill M. Clemens